IMAGES
of America

TEMECULA
WINE COUNTRY

Audrey Cilurzo

Vincenzo

PIONEERS OF THE TEMECULA WINE COUNTRY. Shown from left to right are Nancy and Joe Hart, Audrey Cilurzo, Katharine Filsinger, John Poole, Bridget and Peter Poole, and William Filsinger. Wine Country pioneers not in this photograph are John Moramarco, Vincenzo Cilurzo, Leon Borel, and Dick Break.

ON THE COVER: French Valley neighbors, from left to right, Rosalie Allec Borel, Alexander G. Borel, Pierre Pourroy, and Mary Jaussaud Pourroy pose under vines in this 1930s-era photograph. (Courtesy of Annie Borel.)

IMAGES
of America

TEMECULA
WINE COUNTRY

Rebecca Farnbach,
Vincenzo Cilurzo, and Audrey Cilurzo

ARCADIA
PUBLISHING

Published by Arcadia Publishing
Charleston SC, Chicago IL, Portsmouth NH, San Francisco CA

Printed in the United States of America

Library of Congress Control Number: 2009922885

For all general information contact Arcadia Publishing at:
Telephone 843-853-2070
Fax 843-853-0044
E-mail sales@arcadiapublishing.com
For customer service and orders:
Toll-Free 1-888-313-2665

Visit us on the Internet at www.arcadiapublishing.com

*This book is dedicated to the pioneers of the Temecula Wine
Country, whose vision, dedication, and hard work formed the
foundation for the success of the Wine Country today.*

CONTENTS

ACKNOWLEDGMENTS

We would like to express our appreciation to those individuals who have provided photographs and stories of the Wine Country. We give a big thanks to John and Beverly Moramarco (JBM) for opening their hearts and home to share their stories and their photographs. We also thank Bill Harker (BH) for sharing photographs and stories about the Balloon and Wine Festival, Annie Borel (AB), Roger Honberger (RH), Charlie Curry (CC), Justin Hulse (JH), Paul Gallaher and the *Valley News* (PG, VN), and Darell Farnbach (DF) for contributing their photographs. We appreciate Megan Franks and Sunrise Balloons (MF) and Rudelle Fay Hall (RFH) for their artistic photo-documentation of present-day wineries and the rights to use their photographs. Our thanks go to Bill McBurney for his help with our cover photograph. We also thank the many winery owners who supplied images to demonstrate unique features of their businesses. We appreciate Lisa Woodword's help with Luiseno translation.

All historical images used in this book are from the Cilurzo collection, unless otherwise noted. All modern-day photographs are courtesy of the individual Wine Country business owners, unless other credits are given. If there are people or events not featured in this book, it is because we have attempted to tell the story of the Wine Country within a specified page allotment with the materials at hand.

INTRODUCTION

Vineyards flourish in Temecula because of the ideal climate. In the Luiseno language, *Temecula* means "the place of sun and sand." At an altitude of 1,500 feet, filtered sunlight warms tender plants during the day, and a cool ocean breeze, drifting through a gap in the mountains by late afternoon, coaxes growth from the decomposed granite soil of Temecula Valley. These two factors, the sun and sand, are elements critical to the production of high-quality grapes for premium wines today, as they have been for over a century.

Native Americans who lived in the Temecula Valley enjoyed a diet of abundant game and waterfowl in the verdant land between the many artesian wells. Aged oaks whose toes reached to underground water witnessed generations of native acorn harvests and ceremonial rituals.

Spanish padres discovered the valley in the late 1700s and within a few years began cultivating grain. They also left traces of a few old vines, which most probably produced fruit for sacramental wines. Later French and Italian immigrants nurtured precious vines carried from the Old World, and families fortunate enough to harvest from fledgling family vineyards enjoyed the fruit of the vines at their tables.

In 1889, the Temecula Land and Water Company printed an advertisement stating, "Grapes grow in this valley and all over the foothills, wherever they have been tried, to a remarkable degree of perfection."

During Prohibition, wine making for personal and sacramental uses continued in the Temecula Valley. Although sale of alcohol was forbidden, it was well known that visitors to the Murrieta Hot Springs could connect with a source of wine somewhere in French Valley.

In 1846, Mexican governor of California Pio Pico granted Rancho Pauba, including land that eventually became the Wine Country, to Vicente Moraga. It was ironically later owned for a short time by Luis Vignes, the Frenchman considered the father of California wine making. If Vignes recognized the potential for vineyards, he didn't own the property long enough to plant them. After a short succession of owners, in 1905, Walter Vail purchased Rancho Pauba and combined it with three neighboring ranchos to build an immense cattle empire. In 1964, Kaiser Aetna purchased the 87,500-acre Vail Ranch for $21 million and started to sell plots and parcels in the planned community of Rancho California. Many of the present-day vineyards were originally zoned for citrus.

Vincenzo and Audrey Cilurzo started the Temecula Wine Country. They visited Temecula on their way to Escondido to consider buying a fast-food franchise in 1967, but after speaking with Brack Hale, a real estate salesman for the Kaiser Aetna company, they decided instead to purchase 100 acres for agricultural use.

The town of Temecula had a population of 200 at the time. The Swing Inn was a stop on State Highway 395, and the Long Branch Saloon on Front Street ran a bustling business. The renowned painter Ralph Love's Art Shack, a general store, and a full-service gas station in Old Town Temecula made up the commercial district of Temecula. During this time, there was only one school in Temecula, and after moving here, Audrey served on the Temecula School Board. Citizens of Temecula pooled resources to build a sports park, an effort recognized by Pres. Ronald Reagan in a speech about the "Can Do" spirit.

The Cilurzos hired Dick Break, a viticulture expert with years of experience with grapes in Northern California, who did a feasibility study and determined that Temecula had nearly the same climate as Napa for growing premium varietal wine grapes. Early in 1968, Dick Break supervised Leon Borel to plant virus-free cuttings of Petite Sirah and Chenin Blanc grapes, and this became the first commercial vineyard in the Temecula Valley.

Prior to planting, they prepared the vineyard by digging the soil to a depth of 4 feet to loosen the earth for easier root growth. The vineyard was fenced with barbed wire to keep the roaming cattle out, and chicken wire was inserted to keep rabbits and squirrels from nibbling the tender growth.

During the first summer, an infestation of grasshoppers from Mexico demolished half of the new vines. Dick Break contacted the California Department of Agriculture, and the next morning at dawn an airplane flew over the vineyards spraying malathion. By afternoon, millions of dead grasshoppers covered fields and roadways. Drivers tolerated a strong burnt-coffee smell as their engines roasted the grasshopper carcasses kicked up from the tires. At that time, there was no consideration of malathion's harm to humans, and Audrey Cilurzo and her soon-to-be-born daughter tolerated it well.

During the early years, the Cilurzos performed much of the work in the vineyards when they came down for weekends from their home in Hollywood, where Vincenzo worked as a lighting director for ABC Television network shows. Eventually they moved to Temecula and maintained an apartment in Hollywood until Vincenzo retired. Their children, Vinnie and Chenin, remember playing in the vine rows while Audrey and Vincenzo pruned, trained vines, and did whatever else needed to be done.

As Vincenzo and Audrey learned about the science of grape growing, they freely shared information with other folks who were considering putting in vineyards in the Temecula area. One August day in 1968, Ely Callaway, the president and CEO of Burlington Industries, whose claim to fame was the invention of pantyhose, came to the Cilurzo vineyard dressed in a wool Brooks Brothers suit. He said he had two hours to learn all there was to know about the wine business. Callaway built the first commercial winery in 1975. John Poole started Mount Palomar Winery, and the Cilurzos opened theirs in 1978.

By 1981, there were seven wineries in the Temecula Wine Country. The majority of the wineries didn't charge for tasting, but Callaway charged 25¢ per variety. It took several years before Temecula was recognized as a tourist destination, and several local residents had bumper stickers asking, "Where the hell is Temecula?" As the wineries became better known, tourists began to flock to the area, tasting wine and enjoying musical entertainment offered by wineries. In 1983, the first annual Temecula Valley Balloon and Wine Festival was held on an empty lot in Old Town, an event that now draws as many as 50,000 attendees to Lake Skinner and introduces all of Southern California to the Temecula Wine Country.

The Temecula Wine Country was distinguished as a wine producing area when its appellation became official in 1983. The boundaries of the Temecula Wine Country were defined as the area formerly encompassed by the Vail Ranch.

Local growers initially planted both red and white grapes, but because Ely Callaway was not successful in producing good red wine and said the climate was too hot to grow red grapes, many started growing only white grapes. In 1991, after 60 *Minutes* aired a program called "The French Paradox," which asked why the French who drank red wine had less heart disease than their America counterparts who drank white wine, many growers grafted back to red grapes.

Today there are over 30 wineries. From the beginning, local growers and winemakers have banded together to share ideas and innovations. This has evolved into the Temecula Valley Winegrowers Association. The Temecula Valley Wine Society was also created, not only to educate members, but also to support local wineries and to help with wine competitions.

This book presents the story of the steps taken to develop wines that appeal to the taste of every palate and to market this enjoyable tourist area. Photographs show grazing lands, virgin ground that became the vineyards known today, and the dirt access roads that are now thoroughfares. The processes of grape growing and wine making are shown step by step. The book also introduces the people involved in the Wine Country and sheds light on the business side of the winery business. The last chapter represents wineries in business at the time of compiling this book and shows some of the special features they offer.

Why not pour a glass of Temecula wine and sit in a sunny nook to savor the book and let a little history warm your heart? Salud!

One

THE FIRST VINES

Padres from Mission San Luis Rey brought the first grapes to the area, growing the fruit for sacramental use as well as for their tables. As other Europeans settled the Temecula Valley, they found the climate was similar to the warm regions of Italy and France where they had come from, and they planted tender vines they had carried from the Old Country. It wasn't until 1968 that the Cilurzos planted the first commercial vineyard in the Temecula Valley, starting an industry that is now recognized throughout the state of California and nationwide. Although they encountered challenges of pests and weather during the first few years, the sturdy vines and the farmers persisted until good harvests proved the region as ideal for growing grapes for wine.

MISSION SAN LUIS REY. When Spanish padres founded the mission in 1798, they brought grapevines from stock originating in Spain. By the peak of the mission's influence in 1831, their vines produced 2,500 barrels of wine a year. Temecula Valley was cultivated with grain for the mission, and it is believed that some of the very old grapevines are from mission plantings. (DF.)

OVER 100-YEAR-OLD VINE. The Cilurzos found this old vine on the property they bought on Long Valley Road in 1967 and believe the vine was from a mission grape from vines originally planted by the San Luis Rey padres in the early 1800s. The knobby appearance is due to the head pruning technique used. The Cilurzos made their first wine from this vine's fruit using a wine-making kit purchased from Sears. No one knows how many old vine varieties were grown in the Temecula Valley. Old Zinfandel and mission vines are still found in a few places in the valley. Early families had vines to make wine for their own use. Children were given a few tablespoons of wine and a big glass of water at most meals. By today's standard, those wines were poor quality. However, during Prohibition, when visitors to Murrieta Hot Springs bought bootleg wine, no one complained about the taste.

FELIPE CAZAS'S VINEYARD, PECHANGA. These historic grapevines were originally planted by Felipe Cazas in the late 1800s on 20 acres of the Pechanga Reservation. Two of Felipe's great-grandchildren, Roger Honberger and Patsy Winbury, care for the slightly more than 2 acres of the vineyard that still remain. They say Felipe brought the original plants from Europe after a two-year sojourn with three or four other people from the Temecula area. (RH.)

ESTAFENA CAZAS FREEMAN HOLDING DOROTHY FREEMAN, C. 1923. Estafena, the daughter of Felipe Cazas and Louisa Ayal Cazas of Pechanga, married James Oliver Freeman, who came to California from Texas. James and Estafena lived in the foreman's house at the Vail Ranch while James worked as foreman for the Vail family. Later they lived in their home at the corner of Main and Pujol Streets. The home is still standing. (RH.)

GENE (LEFT) AND PETE ESCALLIER, C. 1983. The two brothers, whose French parents emigrated from Europe, enjoy wine from handblown glasses during a three-day event held at Calloway Winery. The Escallier family owned a pool hall at the northeast corner of Front and Main Streets. An advertisement in the *Wildomar Transcript* newspaper that ran in August 1888 announced "pure wines, liquors, and cigars" were available at the Escallier brothers' business. (JBM.)

THE ESCALLIER BARN IN OLD TOWN TEMECULA. The Escallier Barn is thought to be the first wine storage facility in the Temecula Valley. The granite basement, constructed from stone quarried south of town, kept barrels of wine cool, even during hot summer days. Local historians prompted the saving of the barn, now on Pujol Street, when it was moved to make way for the Temecula City Hall. (DF.)

THE BORELS AND POURROYS. Frenchmen Alexander G. Borel (second from left) and Pierre Pourroy (second from right), some of the first settlers in French Valley in the 1880s, grew grapes and produced up to 200 gallons of wine per year, as allowed during Prohibition. Borel told the Cilurzos that their friend the sheriff would notify them when the marshal was on the way to raid bootleggers. He said the Borels hid all their bottles along the bank of the creek and covered the bottles with straw to look like it was erosion control. They never were caught during Prohibition. The Pourroys had one of the first windmills and an elevated tank to supply running water to the house and yard. This picture shows the men with their wives, Rosalie Borel (left) and Mary Jaussaud Pourroy (right). (AB.)

FRENCH VALLEY WINERY. Leon Borel, the grandson of Alexander Borel, was already experienced and knowledgeable about farming and growing vines for grapes when he worked with Dick Break planting early vineyards. He was a quiet man, so unless someone questioned him, they didn't find out how much he knew about viticulture. He started the French Valley Vineyard in 1984 and closed the winery around 1997. A few old vines stand unattended behind the building today. The distinctive structure is now divided for use by two groups, the Moose Lodge and the Blessed Teresa of Calcutta Catholic Church, both of which serve wine. Leon's grandfather Alexander, a cattle buyer and salesman, came through the area on horseback and decided to start ranching among the other Frenchmen in French Valley in 1886. When Leon died in 1996, he was carried through Old Town Temecula to the cemetery in a horse-drawn wagon with mourners following on horseback and on a hay wagon. (RFH.)

CILURZOS HIKING VIRGIN LAND. Much of the ground in today's wine country was uncultivated until it was planted for vineyards. Early accounts tell of wild oats and chaparral filling spaces between rocks in the valley. Although some of the flat land was cleared of rocks and planted for grain, potatoes, and carrots, much was left undisturbed into the 1980s, when the area was widely planted with citrus and vineyards.

LONG VALLEY ROAD, c. 1967. Long Valley Road, now known as Rancho California Road, was a dusty, rutted, dirt road with a width of 8 feet across that intersected the former Pauba Rancho. Previously a driver had to stop to open and close cattle fences every few miles in the area that seemed so remote from town in those days. The Cilurzos' Jeep was one of the few cars traveling the road back then.

RANCH HOUSE. This old house, one of the few buildings on the 100 acres the Cilurzos purchased in 1967, served as a weekend home until the family moved to Temecula in 1970. To the right was a portable cook shack. During harvest seasons, cooks prepared and served food in the enclosure shielded from bright sunlight and flies. Beyond the cookhouse stood a portable bunkhouse, also designed to transport to the field during harvest.

YODER CAMP. Long before the Cilurzos purchased the property, the Yoders leased it from the Vails. Besides the house and cook shack, there were two big barns, a rustic outhouse, a well, a windmill, and a shed with a copper water tank on the roof where water warmed in the sun. The windmill and one of the barns are still standing at the location know now known as Maurice Car'rie Winery.

YODER CAMP BARN. This barn, still standing, is thought to have been built around 1900. It has a cement floor. From 1905 to 1964, the Vail family owned the property and used the barn for grain storage. M. J. Yoder leased 7,000 acres from the Vails and lived in the farmhouse. Yoder dry farmed, growing grain. He raised barley and paid his lease with one quarter of his grain crop. After the Cilurzos purchased the property, they stored their first vine cuttings inside the barn during the winter of 1967. The flatbed wagon was later moved up the hill, where the Cilurzos used it as a stage for annual grape stomps, with barrels placed on it. The Cilurzos used the barn for dances. Money raised from the barn dances was used to start the road district to improve the dirt roads in Wine Country. The old house and other barn were torn down by Bud and Maurice Van Roekel after they purchased the property in the late 1980s. The Maurice Car'rie Winery now utilizes the barn for weddings and other events.

OFFICIALLY IN BUSINESS. Audrey and Vincenzo Cilurzo shake hands on their agreement to grow grapes on the acres they bought along Long Valley Road, and the posted sign made it official. The emblem at the top of the sign is the Rancho California logo. The area was called Rancho California until voters chose the historical name Temecula when they voted for cityhood in 1989.

DICK BREAK (LEFT) AND VINCENZO CILURZO, 1968. While the Kaiser Development company was planting citrus groves, Break was adamant in his belief that the climate of Temecula was ideal for growing premium varietal grapes. Studies showed strong similarities between temperatures in Temecula and Napa. Over the years, nearly all the citrus groves have been removed and replaced with grapes.

PREPARING THE SOIL. Vincenzo Cilurzo oversaw heavy equipment preparing land for planting. Huge mechanical teeth dug 4 feet into the soil to loosen it so the vines could reach water easily and grow sturdy roots. Grapevines sometimes reach over 30 feet deep for moisture. This was done under the supervision of viticulturist Dick Break. In the 1960s, vines were propagated by buying 18-inch cuttings from a reputable grower who could be trusted to deliver disease-free plants of the variety ordered. Nowadays nurseries sell year-old plants and certify the health and variety ordered. Vines are planted in the soil up to the top bud to develop a good root system. At the end of the first year, the little vine is pruned back severely to encourage the development of good roots. During the second year, there is tremendous growth and the strongest cane is trained up a stake and often along the wire.

PLANTING NEW VINES. The men on the far left and right lined up small wooden pegs to show where cuttings would be planted. Vineyard workers like these often were very experienced and knowledgeable about growing and harvesting grapes. Although much labor was done by hand, at times trucks pulled machinery into the vineyards to dispense wire, fertilizer, or water. The Cilurzos planted the first vineyard in January and February 1968.

STRETCHING WIRE. Workers unrolled wire and attached it to wooden grape stakes, stretching and wrapping the wire around end posts. This was done carefully to prevent damage to the young vines and so stakes would not break. The vines were then trained along the wires to grow both horizontally and vertically. Nowadays metal grape stakes are used.

CHANGING TIMES. Water trucks rolled onto Long Valley Road into the land dominated just a few months before by Vail Ranch cowboys. So little traffic came by that everyone stopped to look at each vehicle passing on the narrow dirt road. Water was used to soften the soil for planting.

IRRIGATION. Hoses and sprinklers were installed to irrigate vineyards. Until the early 1980s, overhead sprinklers were widely used. They are still used in cold areas for spring frost protection, spraying at 15-minute intervals to freeze water around tender leaves and protect them from heavy frost damage. More efficient plastic hose drip systems are popular in most vineyards today, set at 18 to 24 inches above the ground to prevent damage from small animals.

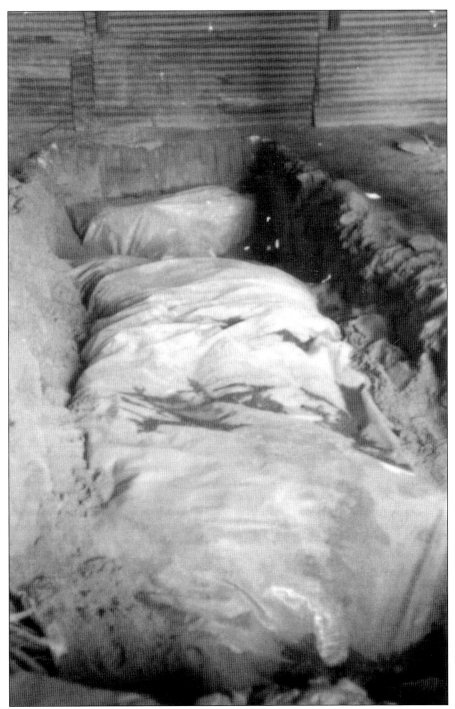

GRAPE CUTTINGS. Eighteen-inch virus-free grape cuttings were wrapped in plastic and set into a wet trench to keep fresh in the barn until planting. The Cilurzos purchased these cuttings in the winter of 1967 from Wente Brothers in Livermore Valley. The Wentes purchased their vines from the neighboring Concannons, who brought their cuttings from Europe. The vines were planted in the early spring of 1968.

VINEYARD RATTLESNAKE. This is a rattlesnake John Moramarco found snuggling against a case of Callaway wine in the 1970s. A king snake devoured the rattlesnake after the photograph was taken. There were more creatures in the wine country in the early days than there are now. The Cilurzos killed 56 rattlesnakes while planting their first 25 acres in 1968. (JBM.)

JOHN MORAMARCO WITH HAWK. Hawks hovering in vineyards reduce populations of critters that damage vines, so growers encourage hawks and owls, sometimes building nests or boxes to invite them to reside nearby. The presence of birds of prey also reduces the population of starlings that eat grapes. Coyotes like the taste of grapes and sometimes chew through irrigation hoses. (JBM.)

SPIDER WEB IN VINE. Insects, although beautiful, can harm grape production. In the 1990s, glassy-winged sharpshooters carried Pierce's Disease, a bacterium that destroys vineyards, to Temecula. The disease was eradicated by working with the California Department of Agriculture in removing diseased vines and by delivering insecticides in air spray and in irrigation water.

SNOW IN THE WINE COUNTRY. In December 1968, a heavy snow covered the entire Temecula Valley 6 inches deep, causing anxiety to farmers and freezing many acres of newly planted orange trees. Kaiser paid citrus growers $5 per tree to replant. This shows the former Yoder Camp, now Maurice Car'rie Winery, under a heavy blanket of snow. The grapevines were dormant and did not suffer damage.

BABY VINES OF CHENIN BLANC. This new baby vine grows by a small peg that will later be replaced by a stake as the vine grows. Wire will be installed between the wood stakes in the vineyard, and the rapidly growing vines will be trained along the wires. Railroad ties were sometimes used for end posts because they could withstand the great weight of the full vines laden with fruit.

ONE-YEAR-OLD VINE. Nowadays a one- to two-year-old rooting is bought from a disease-free certified nursery. In 1968–1969, eighteen-inch cuttings were bought from an existing vineyard and all but the top bud was planted in the ground. This plant was a year old in 1969, when hordes of grasshoppers devoured 51 percent of the vines. During that era, rows were planted far enough apart to allow tractors and other equipment to drive between them.

TRAINING VINES, 1971. Workers trained vines along wires to keep them off the ground. Visitors often were surprised to find seeds when they sampled grapes and found juice from wine grapes much more flavorful than ordinary grape juice. Many vineyard workers came from Mexico and lived in barns on the property until they were needed to help harvests crops for other farmers. Workers sent most of their earnings home to Mexico.

CHENIN CILURZO AND CHENIN BLANC VINES. Two-year-old Chenin Cilurzo stands under a sign denoting a row of Chenin Blanc vines in 1970. She and her husband, Sean Carlton, now live in Pacific City, Oregon, and produce Basket Case Wine and Shy Chenin Wines. Chenin says she is glad her parents didn't grow Gewürztraminer grapes. Vineyards were planted 12 feet wide and 8 feet apart at the time. Today vines are planted closer together and grow higher.

FULL VINES. Leaves are trained to sit in a position to protect ripening grapes from sunburn. Training the vines in the early years helps to determine the shape and strength of the vines for years to come. Young vines are watered often, and weeds that take away moisture from the vine are destroyed. Some growers keep the entire vine row disked, and others leave grasses along the middle of the rows as homes for "good bugs" that help to control pests that try to invade vineyards. Many such techniques were originally taught by Dick Break, an agricultural consultant. Today growers can choose from many clones of the same grape variety. Different clones are better suited to various soils or climates. Also, today DNA testing is done routinely to certify the grape variety. The University of California at Davis has historic nurseries of varieties of grapes grown in the early days of the California wine grape industry.

Two

HARVESTING AND
MAKING WINE

After surviving the challenges of a grasshopper infestation and an invasion of tromping cattle that still roamed the old ranchlands during the first growing season, Cilurzo grapes were ready for picking. The new farmers, guided by experts, yielded a good harvest, and the rest is history. By the time a vine is three years old, it can and will produce about half of its eventual annual capacity. Different varieties of grapes will produce varying amounts of berries when mature. The size of the berries and the size of the bunches vary from variety to variety as well. During the early Temecula harvests, most grapes were picked into field boxes, and later 2-ton gondolas were used. Small wineries utilized volunteers for the first few years, who filled bus trays and dumped them into the de-stemmer/crusher. This was hard and sticky work, especially when the weather was hot, but the quality of the wine proved the hard work was worthwhile.

Rejoicing in Good Vines. Vincenzo Cilurzo showed his pleasure for the warmth of the sunshine and the bountiful growth of his vineyards. When the Cilurzos invested in acreage near Temecula to grow grapes in 1967, they ventured into the unknown. Fortunately for them, and for the many other Wine Country businesses and consumers of Temecula Wine Country products today, their gamble paid off. Vincenzo's parents were proud to visit his vineyard in 1968. Temecula, then wide open and nearly uninhabited, reminded them of the climate and geography of Italy. They emigrated from Sovarato, in Calabria, Italy, to Syracuse, New York, where Vincenzo was born. Audrey Cilurzo, originally from Canada, also loved the climate of sunny warm Southern California, and once she experienced it, she never returned to live in the cold country.

CHECKING SUGAR. Winemaker Chris Stanton checks the amount of sugar in grapes by placing a drop of juice on the glass of a refractometer. Vineyard owners also test sweetness by taste. Wine flavors are maximized when care is given to pick grapes when they reach the desired level of sugar content. The sugar content is measured by percentage of brix. Wine can be made from the juice of many different fruits and plants, including apples, cherries, pears, and dandelions, but it is usually made from grapes. Throughout history, wine has been used in religious rituals and in celebrations. Wine is also used as a beverage and in cooking to flavor food. Grapes for sweet or late harvest dessert wines are allowed to hang on the vines until they are very ripe. After pressing, the juice is fermented in an extremely cold tank, just above freezing. The fermentation may take months. The grower gets fewer gallons of juice from a ton of grapes because of juice lost during the ripening process. Late harvest wines are very expensive.

PICKING CREW, 1974. During the first few harvests, grapes were picked by hand into bus trays. Tractors pulled gondolas through the vineyard, and workers dumped full bus trays into the gondolas. As soon as a gondola was full, the tractor slowly drove the loaded gondola to the winery crusher, where it was emptied. The crew shown here was from Corona. They were hired by Callaway and were given transportation to the Temecula vineyards. Some owners of smaller vineyards do the picking themselves or with the help of volunteers. Often, after crushing the grapes, vintner owners would host barbecues to thank their volunteers. Usually the helpers would also go home with bottles of wine. Many of the volunteers became close friends and continued to help at various events in the Wine Country, including barrel tastings and harvest festivals. (JBM.)

HARVESTING. Workers pick grapes amazingly fast and are sometimes preferred to mechanized harvesters that tend to break the skins of the berries and lose juice and may be destructive to the vines and posts. Many of the workers were highly skilled and returned to the same vineyard every year. One of the Mexican nationals who worked for the Cilurzos put five of his children through college, including his youngest son, who finished medical school. The vineyard workers sometimes also labored with other agricultural commodities besides grapes as the season permitted. As wineries were able to afford larger and better equipment, the harvesting became easier. Less and less hand labor is needed these days. Large wineries had automated equipment from the start, so most harvesting was done by staff. In addition to physical work, much laboratory testing is needed to be sure the wine is stable and ready to drink prior to bottling. (JBM.)

VINEYARD. Gondolas were owned by the vineyards. Painted on their sides were the name of the winery and its weight when empty. When a full gondola is hoisted and weighed, the weight of the empty container is subtracted and the remaining sum is calculated for a selling price of the grapes or to estimate wine yield. Growers are concerned with profit because they also must pay fees. Wineries are assessed by Riverside County, plus they must pay federal and state taxes on every bottle of wine sold. Another annual tax is the $200 assessment on every land parcel in Wine Country for Road District CSA 149 to improve and pave roads. It was thought this would pay for one mile of paving a year. Prices have risen, but nearly all the area roads are paved and maintained. The road district improvements have brought changes from the early days when residents with tractors had to pull customers out of ditches along slippery roads. (JBM.)

PUTTING GRAPES INTO GONDOLA. Juan Rodriguez, an experienced farm laborer, emptied a pan full of harvested grapes into a gondola in the Callaway vineyard. Workers wore gloves, hats, long pants, and long sleeves as protective gear. In 1978, urologist John Piconi, M.D., collaborated with Vincenzo Cilurzo in the Cilurzo-Piconi Winery. The two parties split after a year to start their own wineries. (JBM.)

FIRST CALLAWAY HARVEST, 1973. Instead of filling gondolas, workers loaded the bed of a dump truck with harvested grapes in a Callaway vineyard. The grapes were sold to Brookside Winery in the Ontario area. Vineyard workers often returned to the same vineyard year after year. Shell casings were found throughout the area from artillery practice done during World War II. (JBM.)

GRAPES SENT TO MONDAVI. Thirty-pound boxes of this shipment of grapes that left at dusk arrived fresh at the Mondavi Winery at dawn after driving all night. The Mondavi family, Italian immigrants in the early 1900s, owned a grape wholesale business prior to buying the rundown Charles Krug Winery in Napa in 1943. They renovated the winery from the decades of disrepair and neglect during Prohibition and the Great Depression. The Mondavis innovated the cold fermentation and sterile techniques that are now generally used to produce crisp white wines. Another technique generally used to improve the quality of grapes grown and the quality of wine produced is to analyze grape leaves that fall from each vine after harvest. Vines are pruned and trained to produce the maximum amount of good fruit during the next year. (JBM.)

TRUCKS LEAVING. Petite Sirah grapes were harvested when they were at about 23.5 brix, or percent, sugar. White grapes are picked at lower sugar levels of about 20 to 21 brix and grapes for sparkling wine or champagne are picked at about 18 brix. Nowadays many grapes are harvested at higher sugar levels to increase flavor, which also produces wines of higher alcohol content. (JBM.)

REFRIGERATED TRUCKS. Before the Cilurzo Winery was up and running, they sold Chenin Blanc grapes to the Brookside Winery. They were handpicked and loaded into dump trucks. In this picture, handpicked boxes of grapes from Callaway are being loaded into a refrigerated truck for transport to Napa to be crushed and made into wine. Locally grapes were picked into 1-ton gondolas to prevent damage to the grapes. (JBM.)

GRAPES BY BARN. In the early days, Cilurzo grapes were picked into grape boxes. Here grapes are loaded on the truck from the vineyard. This barn, formerly owned by the Cilurzos, is still being used by Maurice Car'rie Winery. The only man identified in the photograph is John Moramarco, on the right. Some commercial grapes are grown in DeLuz and LaCresta. The Wine Country produces many varieties for wine. Individual wineries have preferences for different varietals, including Cabernet Sauvignon, Chardonnay, Pinot Noir, Riesling, and others. U.S. wine regulations require at least 75 percent of the wine in a bottle be made from the grape named on the label. In the United States, over 85 percent of all wine is produced in California. Historically physicians have prescribed wine as medicine. Today it is touted as a digestive aid and a relaxant and is considered a preventative for cardiovascular disease.

PETITE SIRAH GRAPES. These grapes are ready to be crushed. When the Cilurzos planted the first commercial vineyard in Temecula in 1968, they planted 15 acres of Petite Sirah and 25 acres of Chenin Blanc. Three months later, Brookside Winery planted a vineyard in the Temecula Valley, but irrigation problems caused them to lose much of the planting. This variety can rot if it is too wet. Petite Sirah grapes were originally produced as a cross between Syrahs and Durifs to produce more mildew-resistant fruit. This variety gives heavy yields of 4 to 6 tons per acre. The fruit produces tight clusters of grapes. The vines are sturdy and have longevity. The Cilurzos were charter members of the Petite Sirah growers and winemakers association, called "P.S. I Love You." (Petite Sirah, I Love You). More and more wineries are making Petite Sirah wine each year. Petite Sirahs are full bodied, complex, and have deep color and a peppery flavor.

FILLING TRAYS FOR THE CRUSHER. In the early days, before many wineries could afford to buy automated equipment, much of the work was done by hand. This image shows family and volunteers filling bus trays with grapes and then dumping them into the crusher in the background. Leaves and stems were discarded, and the grapes were sent into the winery to be pressed and to have the juice fermented into wine. Stems were scattered through the vineyard to become mulch. Chenin Cilurzo (standing on the tire) and her brother Vinnie (center) pitch in to help in this photograph. The Cilurzos' German foreign exchange student Gerti Mader is at the crusher. She enjoyed her new experiences learning firsthand about growing grapes, using mulch to produce natural nitrogen fertilizer, and making wine. Loyal friends who came year after year to help harvest grapes and bottle wine enjoyed a barbecue afterward. Grapes are often picked during the night when it is cool. Cooler grapes make better wine. Gondolas are delivered to wineries at dawn, and grapes are usually crushed and put into cold tanks before noon.

Weighing the Full Gondola. The weight of an empty gondola is subtracted from its full weight to determine the tonnages of grapes being purchased and to give the winemaker an estimate of his potential wine production and the amount of yeast needed to ferment the grapes. Gondolas usually hold about 2 tons of grapes, but sizes may vary by winery. Grapes grow in clusters with as few as 6 and as many as 300 berries. In 2007, the Wine Institute reported sales of 554 million gallons of California wine in the United States and abroad. Fossils of grape leaves and seeds indicate human consumption of grapes since prehistoric times. The earliest evidence of cultivation of grapes is found in ancient Egyptian drawings from approximately 2440 BC. Babylonians and Chinese also recorded early use of wine.

GRAPES IN THE CHUTE. Vincenzo Cilurzo checks the quality of the fruit as the grapes are raked from the gondola into the de-stemmer/crusher below. The stems are then hauled to the vineyard and spread along vine rows as mulch and to fertilize the vines. The berries are broken so the juice will run. Berries are pumped into the winery to be pressed or pumped into a tank to ferment. Often the berries sit in cold tanks to pick up flavors before pressing or fermenting, a process called a cold soak. Red berries are pumped into a tank where yeast is added and the whole berry is fermented. Some refrigeration is used to prevent the fermenting fruit from getting too warm. The alcohol level is checked every day until all the natural sugar from the berries is converted into alcohol and the juice has been transformed into wine. Then the wine pulp and skins are pumped into a press where the wine is gently pressed away from the skins and seeds. Juice from red grapes is put into barrels to age for about a year.

A Full Bus Tray. Mike Westman and his wife, Sue, both retired officers of the U.S. Air Force, always volunteered to help. Mike is shown here with a loaded bus tray to be dumped into the de-stemmer/crusher. If the grape is red, the entire berry is put into a tank. If it is white, the berry is pressed and only the juice is slowly fermented at a cold temperature.

Processing Grapes, Early 1980s. Vinnie Cilurzo (left) fills trays, while winemaker Mike Tingley dumps trays full of Chenin Blanc grapes into the de-stemmer being run by Vincenzo Cilurzo in this labor-intensive process. Stems, seeds, and skins were then loaded into wheelbarrows to spread as mulch in the vineyards. Tingley is the Keyways winemaker now.

INTO THE CRUSHER. Volunteer Mike Westman and winemaker Karen Vandervort work at the crusher. After the stems were removed, red grapes were pumped through hoses into tanks in the winery. Leftover stems and skin are called "pumice." Quality wines can be produced without a lot of equipment. Needed are good grapes, good weather, properly used sanitary equipment, and a passion for fine wine.

EARLY EQUIPMENT. Here red grapes are being crushed. Red grapes are fermented on their skins and then pressed. White grapes go into a press to extract juice from the skins, and the juice is pumped into a tank to ferment at a cold temperature of approximately 50 degrees Fahrenheit.

MORE MODERN CRUSHER. Chrissy Stanton and Eric Cilurzo work at the de-stemmer/crusher. Small wineries added equipment as funds permitted. When more efficient machinery was purchased, this made the process faster, but some volunteers thought it wasn't nearly as fun as the older, more primitive methods. If white grapes are crushed, the stems are removed and the berries are pressed before putting the juice into a very cold tank, where the fermentation is cold and slow. The skins and seeds left after pressing are called pumice. It is spread along the vine rows as fertilizer. Generally white wine needs little time in the bottle before it is ready for sale, but red wine generally requires aging in barrels before it is sold. Colonists found wild grapes when they arrived in the eastern United States, but they were unsuccessful with cultivation until the late 1700s.

GRAPE PRESS. Winemaker Mike Tingley oversees the press while Vinnie Cilurzo and an unidentified volunteer load it with grapes. Grapes are slowly and gently pressed, and the juice drips into a large pan beneath the press. If the pressing is too hard, bitter tannins and off flavors go into the wine. The juice is then pumped into refrigerated tanks to be fermented into wine to further prepare it for bottling. Historically grapes were crushed by stomping on them, an act that is re-created during harvest festivals. Also, large mechanized presses were used in California missions. With those presses, a person lowered thick wooden plates into barrels of grapes by turning a heavy crank. Often the barrel would have a spout from which the wine would pour into a pottery bottle. Many of those presses are on display in museums and in the missions.

FILTERS. Before wine is bottled, it is pumped through a series of filters to remove sediment to produce clear and brilliant wine. A natural plankton or algae product called diatomaceous earth coats each plate in the filter, and the wine is gently pumped through the plates. The sediment is left behind. This photograph shows Vincenzo Cilurzo checking hoses on the filter. Equipment requires constant observation, maintenance, and repair to keep it running and sanitary. Winemakers pride themselves in the vigilant care they give to their products, from the vine to the bottle, monitoring each step to produce the flavor, body, and aroma that showcase their wines and delight the palate. Frank Burnham described how in the early 1900s Jack and Pete Escallier would tromp on grapes in a horse trough resting on two sawhorses. They would save the juice and discard the remainder behind buildings in Old Town Temecula, where it would ferment and attract all the loose livestock. After partaking of the fermenting mess, the animals amused observers watching them stagger down Main Street.

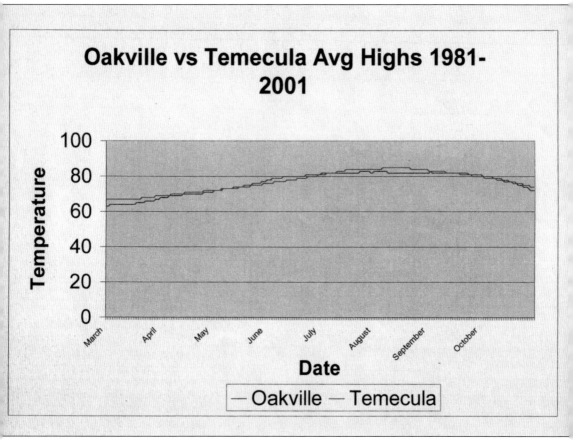

Oakville vs Temecula Avg Highs 1981-2001

Oakville — Temecula

TEMPERATURE COMPARISON. Before the first commercial vineyard was planted in 1968, Dick Break insisted the Temecula Valley was not too hot for grapes. This 1981 comparison, done in 1981 by Sean Carlton, Vincenzo and Audrey Cilurzo's son-in-law, demonstrates nearly identical temperatures during the growing season in Temecula Valley and Oakville in the Napa Valley. Too warm a climate makes the sugar content in the grapes overpower the acidity. Surprisingly, during some growing seasons, the Temecula Valley is actually cooler than some Northern California growing areas. The ocean breeze that flows through the Rainbow Gap every afternoon regulates the valley's warmer daytime temperatures. The breeze gives the Temecula Valley the breath of fresh air that makes all the difference. Many grapes in the Temecula Valley are picked at night. Powerful lights above the tractors and gondolas illuminate the vineyards, making an eerie sight in low-lying fog. Cold grapes make better wine, and by picking at night the workers have fewer insects to contend with.

MAKING NOUVEAU BEAUJOLAIS WINE. Whole bunches of red grapes are put into tanks, and the tanks are then sealed to let the whole berries ferment in their skins. Here John Gleason and Karen Vandervort load Petite Sirah grapes inside the tank. In France, red Nouveau wines are released on the third Thursday of November and are drunk within six months of bottling. Five Temecula wineries made Nouveau wines for a few years, and children of vintners participated in a multi-skill race, as they do to celebrate Nouveau wine production in France. In 1980, the Cilurzos made Gamay Beaujolais wine from a grape related to the Pinot Noir grapes. It was fruity, youthful, snappy, and refreshing with a recognizable aroma and flavor. Wines made in the Beaujolais region of France are typically bright ruby red in color, are full of depth, and have a light body and definitively dry character. They are best served slightly chilled. Made to drink within the first few months of bottling, nouveau wines lose their attributes as they age.

PUNCHING DOWN THE SKINS. While fermenting red wines, the skins tend to rise to the top of the liquid, so they are pushed back down into the tank either by hand or by pumping juice from the bottom over the top and back into the tank. This is usually done about four times a day. Here Eric Cilurzo punches the skin cap back down into the juice to allow the maximum color and complexity to be transferred from the skins into the fermenting juice. The temperature of the mixture is controlled by the thermostat and is insulated by the jacket around the tank. Vincenzo Cilurzo quotes the anonymous rhyme, "White wine is fine, red wine is divine." Rose wines are given shorter time exposure to the skins than red wines.

CLARIFYING WHITE WINE. Vinnie Cilurzo (left) assists winemaker Mike Tingley in separating fresh egg whites from the yolks. Egg whites are mixed in white wine to remove nearly invisible proteins. The proteins cling to the egg whites and drop to the bottom of the tank. If this is not done, the proteins can make the wine cloudy. There is no egg taste to the wine after this process. This is sometimes called a "fining" process. Some vintners use a different "fining agent" such as milk solids or gelatin, a protein substance that clarifies the wine and extracts unwanted tannins and other substances. This slow, deliberate extracting process usually takes a month or so to complete. Sediment and pulp residue that settles in tanks of fermenting juice are called the "lees." Sometimes the sediment is spun out by centrifugal force.

FILLING BARRELS. Mike Tingley pumps wine from a tank into barrels to age and pick up a slight taste of oak. White wines are aged in French Oak barrels, and red wines are aged in American Oak or more expensive French Oak. After five years, barrels become neutral and no longer flavor wine, but barrels can be shaved and the newly exposed wood can give flavor for another five years.

TOPPING THE BARRELS, 1978. Dr. John Piconi uses a makeshift device to replenish the inch or so of wine that evaporated each month from barrels. The Cilurzos started the first commercial vineyard in 1968. Callaway opened the first winery in 1975. Vincenzo Cilurzo and John Piconi bottled 200 cases each of Cabernet Sauvignon and Petite Sirah in 1978. Piconi started his own winery in 1982.

BLENDING WINES. Here Mike Tingley blends wines from several barrels in the cool and humid barrel room prior to preparing the wine for bottling. Blending is done to produce the best possible product from the available wines. Enology is the study of wine and wine making. University of California Davis and California State, Fresno offer bachelor's degrees in viticulture and enology. The Temecula Wine Country produces about 10,000 tons of grapes a year. Some years, grapes give a lighter yield but a better quality, as in the 2008 harvest. The grapes are picked at night or early in the morning, when their quality is the highest, also giving field workers relief from daytime heat and sun exposure. Spring rains are sometimes responsible for reduced yields because the force of heavy rain can knock blooms from vines. Excessive heat can cause vines to stop growing larger fruit to preserve and protect the fruit already on the vines.

Tasting. Vincenzo Cilurzo (left) and Mike Tingley taste a Petite Sirah blend prior to bottling. Tingley made several blends and placed them in wine glasses, recording the percentages of amounts from the various barrels. After deciding on the best blend, the wine is prepared for bottling. When asked which of the Temecula wines is the best wine, most of the vintners say, "Whichever one you like the best." John Moramarco explains that everyone's palate is individual, that some like sweet wines and others prefer dry wines. He says there are many good wines produced in the Temecula Valley, and he has several favorites made by several different wineries. By the sixth year after planting, a vine achieves maturity and produces grapes with full flavor. Grapes need enough sun exposure to ripen, but not too much or they will sunburn.

ITALIAN BOTTLING LINE. After many years of slow, labor-intensive bottling of wine by hand, the sophisticated, Italian-made automatic bottling machine was a welcome change, making the entire process easier and faster. Here Vincenzo Cilurzo monitors the mechanized bottling, making sure the fill level is right as bottles pass through the line.

BOTTLING LINE. A bottle is automatically filled as it comes down the line. Air is sucked out from the top space and the fill level is inspected. Even in a mechanized process, human inspection is needed. Here Vincenzo Cilurzo monitors the corking machine. Vincenzo and Audrey worked in their vineyard and winery while Vincenzo continued his career as a television lighting director, working with ABC Television, Merv Griffith, Joey Bishop, and Frank Sinatra. Vincenzo earned two Emmys for his lighting work in Hollywood.

Automatic Corker. Maria Castaneda places bottles on the bottling line. After passing through the filler, bottles were corked, capsules were spun on, labels were attached, and the bottles were inspected before boxing. Bottles were inserted upside down in the cases to keep the corks moist.

Labeling. Joe Vera (left), winemaker Benny Rodriguez, and volunteers label newly bottled wine. The wine industry, regulated by the Federal Bureau of Alcohol, Tobacco, and Firearms, must list several items on bottle labels, including alcohol content. Before marketing wines, labels must be submitted for federal government approval and must meet certain criteria and laws.

STACKING CASES. Eric Cilurzo, cellar master, stacks cases of newly bottled wine. Since inventory is taken each month to report to the federal government for tax assessment, it is very important to stack wine cases for counting and easy reading of the labels. Wine case labels show the name of the winery, the size of the bottles, how many bottles are in each case, and the date of bottling. Wine bottle labels tell the brand name and the vintage date. The label must show the appellation or region where the grapes making up 75 percent or more of the wine were grown. It must also list the trade name and address of the bottler or exporter. The alcohol content must be listed. A wine with 7 to 14 percent alcohol content may be listed as a "table wine" or "light wine." Varietal designations must be printed to give an idea of what flavor is expected. If the label does not list a percentage of varietal designation, it is at least 75 percent of the variety listed.

SHAVING BARRELS. The insides of oak barrels are shaved after five years of use because the barrels become neutral after giving flavor to wine. Shaving is a special art and people who do this travel from winery to winery. The head, or end, of the barrel is removed, and a router shaves one-fourth to one-half inch of neutral oak from the inside of the barrel to expose new oak. The head is also shaved and put back on the barrel, which is good for another five years. Usually barrels can be shaved twice. Barrels cost hundreds of dollars each, with French Oak barrels being the costliest. American Oak gives stronger flavors. White wines and some red wines are aged in French Oak barrels, which give more subtle flavors. There is a trend to age Belgian-style craft beers in oak barrels.

BARRELS FOR FLAVOR. The main differences between French Oak and American Oak barrels are in their wood density and method of construction. Wood in French Oak barrels comes from five forests originally planted to supply material for building Napoleon's ships. These woods are extremely tight-grained to prevent evaporation and to give maximum flavor to the wine.

NUMBERED PIECES. Before shaving, barrel ends are removed and numbered so they will be reunited after shaving. The barrels may be of different ages or configurations, so they may not fit with other ends. Besides shaving wood to release more flavor into aging wines, some vintners use oak shavings in a bag, like a tea bag, or they use oak pieces to infuse flavor into wines during fermentation in stainless steel tanks.

COOPERAGE. A barrel maker or repairer is called a cooper. His products are called cooperage. French coopers air dry their wood for at least 24 months before using it, but their American counterparts, more in the practice of making whiskey kegs, usually dry their wood in kilns. Europeans make their staves, the slats of wood forming the sides of barrels, by splitting the wood along the grain, while Americans usually saw staves. Barrels may vary in shape according to use. For example, there is a traditional shape used for Bordeaux wines that is slightly different from the usual shape for Burgundy wines. The thickness of the staves may also vary. Barrels are charcoal toasted to a desired depth to produce flavors. Deeper toasting produces stronger flavors. Light to medium toasting produces flavors of coconut or vanilla, while heavy toasting infuses coffee, spice, or caramel flavors and is best suited for bold, red wines.

Three

THE WINERY BUSINESS

For a long time, few people knew about Temecula's vineyards and wineries, but by the late 1980s, the word was out and the Temecula Wine Country was a popular tourist destination. This didn't just happen; it came about because of some colorful, dedicated, and determined individuals. Ely Callaway was a marketing genius whose innovative ideas transformed the American wine industry. Evelyn Harker founded the annual Balloon and Wine Festival and marketed it to all of Southern California, making it an event that attracts thousands of visitors each year. The growers' techniques and care producing quality grapes and the award-winning wines put the Wine Country on the map. Along the way, several remarkable individuals nodded their approval to Temecula Valley Wines and dubbed the region the "New Wine Country." These stories and others are presented in this chapter.

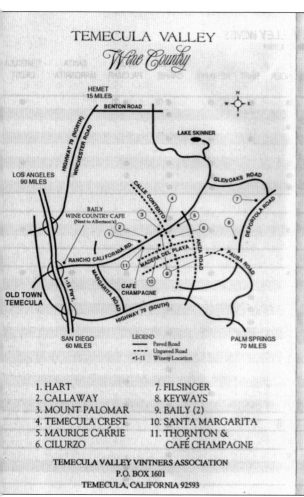

TEMECULA VALLEY
Wine Country

HEMET
15 MILES

BENTON ROAD

HIGHWAY 79 (NORTH)

WINCHESTER ROAD

LAKE SKINNER

GLENOAKS ROAD

LOS ANGELES
90 MILES

CALLE CONTENTO

DE PORTOLA ROAD

BAILY
WINE COUNTRY CAFE
(Next to Albertson's)

RANCHO CALIFORNIA RD.

MADERA DEL PLAYA

ANZA ROAD

PAUBA ROAD

CAFE
CHAMPAGNE

MARGARITA ROAD

I-15 FWY.

OLD TOWN
TEMECULA

HIGHWAY 79 (SOUTH)

SAN DIEGO
60 MILES

LEGEND
— Paved Road
---- Unpaved Road
#1-11 Winery Location

PALM SPRINGS
70 MILES

1. HART
2. CALLAWAY
3. MOUNT PALOMAR
4. TEMECULA CREST
5. MAURICE CARRIE
6. CILURZO

7. FILSINGER
8. KEYWAYS
9. BAILY (2)
10. SANTA MARGARITA
11. THORNTON &
    CAFÉ CHAMPAGNE

TEMECULA VALLEY VINTNERS ASSOCIATION
P.O. BOX 1601
TEMECULA, CALIFORNIA 92593

TEMECULA VALLEY WINES
Available as of March 1, 1994

THE TEMECULA WINE COUNTRY IN 1994. The Temecula Valley Vintners Association published this brochure advertising 11 wineries and one restaurant in 1994. Now a destination for wine connoisseurs, the Temecula Wine Country features over 30 independent wineries and many restaurants that attract visitors from all over the world. The brochure listed eight varieties of white wines, four roses, nine reds, one sparkling, and three dessert wines produced in the Temecula Valley. The Culbertsons specialized in sparkling wines, and Mount Palomar was the only winery making sherry. Filsinger, Baily, Maurice Car'rie, and Mount Palomar Wineries also produced sparkling wines. The Cilurzos were the only people making and producing Petite Sirah in the early days. Most of the wineries bottled both red and white varieties, with Chardonnay and Sauvignon Blanc leading in the white varieties and Cabernet Sauvignon leading in red. White Zinfandel was the favored rose. The unique microclimate, with warm and sunny days cooled by ocean breezes by late afternoon, combines with rich soil to produce award-winning grapes and quality wines.

WINERY OWNERS, LATE 1990s. Winery owners raising glasses at Thornton Winery are, from left to right, Bill Hart, Peter Poole, Carl Keys, John Thornton, Bud and Maurice Von Roekel, Vincenzo Cilurzo, Marshall Stuart, Carol Baily, John Moramarco, and Phil Baily. Wine and grape growers met on a monthly basis to discuss business and marketing. (JBM.)

SAMPLING AT THORNTON WINERY. This photograph captures three men who significantly contributed to early Temecula wine history. From left to right are John Moramarco, Vincenzo Cilurzo, and Philo Biane. Biane owned Brookside Winery in Guasti, and when he bought land in Temecula in 1967, he hired Moramarco to manage the planting of his vineyards. Moramarco later worked for Callaway Vineyards and Winery. Moramarco eventually became vice president of Callaway.

WOMEN OF THE WINE COUNTRY. From left to right are Nancy Hart, Bridget Poole, Carol Baily, Audrey Cilurzo, and Martha Culbertson. All winery owners, each cooked a special dish to serve at a Temecula Valley Wine Society dinner held at Baily Winery in the early 1980s. The society was established in 1982 to support local wineries and to provide volunteers for competitions and other events. Audrey was later awarded a Woman of Merit Award by the *North County Times* newspaper.

CALLAWAY EXECUTIVES. From left to right, Mike Jellison (director of operations for Callaway's parent company, Allied Domecq) meets with John Moramarco, Ely Callaway, and Jon Moramarco, John's son. John Moramarco's father and three uncles made wine in Italy. They came to the United States hoping to make some money before returning to Italy but were lured to California, where they eventually became winemakers at Old Mission Winery in Los Angeles. As a child, John began cultivating vineyards with horses and mules at his family's winery. From 1942 to 1967, John managed the Capistrano Winery vineyards in Fontana, owned by his family. In 2002, John received a lifetime achievement award from the Temecula Valley Chamber of Commerce for his work in developing the Temecula Wine Country. He says, "Water separates people, but wine brings people together," and "[in Temecula] regardless of what the weather is, it is a beautiful day." (JBM.)

Wine Country

These wines were produced within a 10 minute drive of Rancho California's Industrial/Commercial areas.

PROMOTING THE WINE COUNTRY. Many marketing publications advertised the benefits of living and working in the planned community of Rancho California during the era between the selling of the Vail Ranch in 1964 to Kaiser Aetna and Temecula becoming a city in 1989. Given a vote, the growing population chose the historical name of Temecula instead of the cumbersome name of Rancho California, California. This undated brochure published by KACOR (Kaiser Aluminum and Chemical Corporation) emphasized the Wine Country but also mentioned the residential, commercial, agricultural, recreational, and industrial properties available. Only seven wineries were in existence at the time of its publication: Hart, Callaway, Piconi, Mount Palomar, Filsinger, Clos du Muriel, and Cilurzo. Inside it states, "Forget a trip to Napa Valley; seven wineries in nearby Temecula are producing award winning wines" and "meet a group of interesting, independent people who are California's new breed of winemakers."

CALLAWAY VINEYARD CREW, 1985. Callaway employed vineyard workers year-round to perform various duties. They wore hats, long sleeves, and long pants to protect themselves from insects, snakes, and too much sun exposure. Ely Callaway planted the 105-acre vineyard in 1969, and the first wine was made in 1974. Turning a quick profit was important to Ely, so he specialized in white wines that took less time for fermentation. Callaway produced Sweet Nancy, a dessert wine that, when questioned, Ely said was named in honor of Nancy Reagan, and he didn't mention his recent ex-wife, Nancy. Hiram Walker and Sons, known as distillers, bought the property in 1981 and later turned it over to the Allied Domecq division of the company. In 2005, a private party purchased Callaway Vineyards and Winery. The winery continues to thrive under new ownership. (JBM.)

Leon Borel. Leon, hired by Dick Break to plant the Cilurzos' original vineyard, came from an old-time French Valley family. He later planted his own vineyard and started French Valley Winery on Winchester Road, now the Moose Lodge. He is standing here in the doorway of the lower level of the Cilurzo Winery right after crushing. Winery owners were proud to display a Wine Institute sign like the one to his left.

THE WINE INSTITUTE. After the repeal of Prohibition, each state dictated regulations regarding kinds of wines, labels, and containers. The complex regulations differed widely and were difficult to understand, so compliance was difficult. In 1934, the Wine Institute, an advocate for wine business, was formed, which now represents 1,100 wineries and wine-related businesses around the world. This organization influences public policy to the businesses.

PUBLICIZING THE WINE COUNTRY. Bob Balzer (left), who wrote a column about wine for the *Los Angeles Times*, interviewed Ely Callaway. Callaway was largely responsible for the publicity the Wine Country received during the early years. Advertisements showing Callaway sitting in the lead car of six Volkswagen bug vehicles driving in his vineyard were featured in *Newsweek, US News and World Report, Time, Sunset,* and other national magazines. (JBM.)

CELEBRATION AT CALLAWAY. Callaway employees celebrate the 20-year anniversary of the company's purchase by Hiram Walker and Sons in 2001. From left to right are Beverly Stureman (now Moramarco), David Castro, Jose Ceja, Ely Callaway, unidentified winemaker, Art Villareal, John Moramarco, Ramon Ortega, Craig Weaver, and Jon Moramarco. (JBM.)

CALLAWAY SALES TEAM. At a time when wine sales were dominated by male winery representatives, Ely Callaway found a winning combination with his nearly all-female sales force. Pictured from left to right are Beverly Stureman (who later married John Moramarco), Sioux MacLachlin, Christine Snow, Catherine O'Donnell, Eileen Lord, Alis Demoor Arrowhood, Jim Russell, unidentified, Wendy Burns, Donna Gable, and Toni Chase. (JBM.)

ELY CALLAWAY. When Callaway died in 2001, he had been married four times and had succeeded in three careers. *Forbes* magazine called him "a natural huckster" in the way he found innovative products and marketed them. After selling Callaway Winery to Hiram Walker distillers, he invented the Big Bertha golf club, which became the best-selling golf club in history. Former presidents Bill Clinton and George Bush Sr. use Callaway clubs.

JOHN AND MARTHA CULBERTSON. From left to right, a representative for Harry Winston Jewelers of New York, Martha, and John share glasses of Culbertson Blanc de Noir in Tokyo. The Culbertsons were transported to Tokyo on Air Force One for a presidential trade mission. Culbertson's champagne was served for two state dinners at the White House in 1986 and was the official wine of the American Orient Express train.

JULIA CHILD IN TEMECULA. Julia Child and her husband, Paul, visit the Culbertsons' Temecula winery. Shown from left to right are Scott and Julie Culbertson, Paul and Julia Child, Martha and John Culbertson, and John Tyler Culbertson. The Culbertsons, Julia Child, and other people in the food and wine world often met at Culbertson Winery.

CULBERTSONS AND AWARDS. The Culbertsons won numerous awards for their sparkling wines. Jon McPherson was their winemaker. Culbertson Brut has a fruity, fresh yeast aroma after aging for 18 months. Culbertson Blanc de Noir, made from 90 percent Pinot Noir and 10 percent Chardonnay, has a deep fruity character, a floral fragrance, and a hint of strawberry and yeast flavor.

CULBERTSON FOUNTAIN. To market wine products, wineries design romantic nooks for dining and sampling wine, where customers can escape their everyday worries and create magical moments to remember later. The warm memories customers experience bring them back to the winery for more good times. The Culbertsons started the first restaurant, jazz concerts, champagne, and cooking classes in the Temecula Wine Country.

BALLOONING IN THE WINE COUNTRY. The same climate that allows production of quality grapes is also ideal for hot air ballooning. Ballooning brought customers to wine country. The many balloonists and their passengers returned from early morning flights to spend the rest of the day tasting wine. The sky was filled with balloons every weekend morning. (CC.)

BALLOONS AT CILURZOS' POOL. For over 25 years, balloons took off from behind the Cilurzos' pool and adobe house. Residents sometimes complained about being awakened by the sounds of gas burners early on weekend mornings. The balloonists would return with their passengers for a catered brunch at the Cilurzos' home after flights because there were few restaurants in Temecula at the time. Balloons now take off from La Cereza and Maurice Car'rie Wineries.

TEMECULA BALLOON AND WINE FESTIVAL. The annual event was started in 1983 by Evelyn Harker and balloonist Walt Darren as a fund-raiser for the Temecula Chamber of Commerce. In the early years, the event was held in various locations around Temecula. In the 1990s, the festivals moved to Lake Skinner, where 30 to 50 balloons rise, filling the sky and flying where the wind currents carry them. (BH.)

BALLOON OVER LAKE SKINNER. Volunteers Sue and Mike Westman take time off from pouring in tasting booths to take a ride. After dark on Friday evenings of the festivals, balloonists inflate their tethered balloons and light the burners to illuminate the balloons like gigantic Chinese lanterns for the Balloon Glow event. Hundreds of spectators come to hear music and to see the beautifully colored balloons lighting the evening sky.

Barrels Ready for Grape Stomp. Barrels sit on the Cilurzos' flatbed hay wagon overlooking a sky full of hot air balloons in the Temecula Wine Country. The wagon was left from the Vail Ranch that dominated the region until 1964. During harvest time, grape stomps are popular. Many participants say they were inspired by an *I Love Lucy* episode. While one member of a team smashes grapes by stomping on them, the extracted juice pours out a spout into a bottle. The second person holds and fills the bottle. The team that fills their bottle first wins a medal and a bottle of wine. Wineries offer many events to attract the public, which then boosts sales. Crowds of visitors enjoy watching grape stomping during annual harvest festivals at several of the wineries in the Temecula Valley.

BACK SIDE OF STOMPING. Sweet and sticky juice squishes between the toes and up the legs of enthusiastic barefoot stompers, whose movements are like a choreographed dance. Boisterous onlookers cheer on their favorite teams until the winner is announced and the stompers wash the purple juice from their skin. Experienced stompers often bring a change of clothing. Harvest festivals are events to bring visitors to the Wine Country for a fun weekend and to sample various wines produced in the area. Many go home with a case or two of favorite wines. Often members of the Temecula Valley Wine Society volunteer their time to promote the wineries during the festivals. The festivals offer barbecues and musical entertainment. Some participants come year after year to engage in the fun of harvest festival activities. (JBM.)

MUSICAL ENTERTAINMENT. Music and wine go together to make a relaxing good time. The Balloon and Wine Festival always attracts big-name entertainers to draw crowds, and several wineries offer music during harvest festivals and at other times. During nearly every weekend, at least one winery hosts a charity event featuring well-known performers and the pairing of food and wine. Continuing the jazz concert tradition started by the Culbertsons, Steve Thornton, president of Thornton Winery, continued hosting concerts in 1988. At first, the smooth jazz music attracted about 60 patrons, but the crowd runs about 600 today. Nineteen concerts were staged in seven wineries in the fall of 2008, with a star performers list including Kris Kristofferson, Benise, and Dave Koz. Many other musical events were held in the Wine Country to raise funds for charities, including help for children with autism and juvenile diabetes, and for organizations including the Sunrise Rotary Club, the California Family Life Center, and the Unforgettables Foundation. Linda Peace and her band are playing at Cilurzo Winery in this photograph.

ART IN THE VINEYARDS. During harvest festivals and at other times, local artists show their work and offer it for sale. Here Bea Taylor, dressed in a prairie dress and sunbonnet, shows her original paintings. Each year, artists enter a very competitive poster contest for the Balloon and Wine Festival. The Maurice Car'rie Winery allows artisans to rent booth space each weekend where they can show artwork and handcrafted wares, including jewelry, yard art, and birdhouses.

DANCING AND DINING. Music and good food abound at harvest festivals and the Balloon and Wine Festival. And sometimes the music is so good, a person just has to get up and dance. Individual wineries plan special menus for harvest festivals. The Cilurzos sometimes roasted a pig on a spit to serve succulent pork to customers. Many food venders present their wares at the Balloon and Wine Festival, offering cuisine of many ethnicities.

BOCCE. Several wineries have bocce courts for outdoor Italian bowling. Participants throw balls with the object of getting the closest to a white ball on the court. Individual wineries tailor specific activities for groups who make advance arrangements to visit. For example, the Cilurzo Winery hosted the Lamborghini Club of America several times, closing the picnic area for the private barbecue and an afternoon of planned activities, including playing bocce.

TASTING IN BARREL ROOM. Winery owners often invite their wine club members or other special groups to a barrel tasting party. Wines are poured directly from barrels to savor with food that is specially selected to correspond with the wines. These events in the dark, moist, and aromatic barrel rooms are long remembered.

NOUVEAU RACE. The Temecula Valley Wine Society hosted this event in which children of Temecula winery owners raced with nouveau wine through the vineyards, carrying a glass of wine on a tray, and paddled across a pond with a bottle of wine in a boat. Traditionally nouveau wines are released on the third Thursday of November. The children represented the Mount Palomar, Baily, Maurice Car'rie, and Cilurzo Wineries.

NOUVEAU FINISH LINE. The flag bearer signals the finish line at the end of the obstacle race. One of the contestants was Vinnie Cilurzo, who went on to become a world-class brewer. He established the Blind Pig Brewery in Temecula and the Russian River Brewing Company in Santa Rosa, California. One of his signature beers is Pliny the Elder. Vinnie met his wife, Natalie Nichols, when she worked at Hart Winery.

WINERY TOURS. To promote their businesses, wineries offer tours and sample tastes of their products. Here John Moramarco (right) gives a Callaway vineyard tour. Tours usually end in tasting rooms. Most wineries hold special dinners and barrel tasting parties and often host charity events. Many have large wine clubs that promote winery activities and give discounts to members. Winery gift shops sell an array of wine-related items. (JBM.)

TASTING BAR. This image shows Phil and Carol Baily serving visitors in Baily's tasting room. Early on, tasting was free, but Ely Callaway set a precedent when he started charging a minimal fee. Now all wineries charge $5 to $10 for a specified number of tastes. In the past, winery owners poured for seated customers, but they have found it is more practical to serve from a bar.

PICNICS. This image shows a picnic at Cilurzo's pond. Picnic areas are available at nearly every winery, where visitors can enjoy some sunshine and fresh air while tasting wine and cheese. People bring picnics or purchase items from winery delicatessen counters. For many visitors, it is traditional to partake of a meal with a bottle of wine shared among friends to make the winery experience complete. For those who do not want to prepare food or to picnic, an alternate of outdoor restaurant dining is available at many wineries. Maurice Car'rie is famous for its Brie cheese with sourdough bread, enjoyed with a bottle of their wine. People visit the Wine Country to unwind from their usual hectic schedules. Winery owners encourage people to linger, to taste, and to renew their spirits with the beauty around them.

WEDDINGS. Most wineries offer inside and outside wedding venues. In fact, weddings are big business in the Wine Country. Every spring, a wedding fair is held to acquaint brides with the venues and services available in the Wine Country. Many wineries offer wedding planners and supply wedding packages that may include musicians, photographers, clergy, and catering. Facilities of different sizes are available to wedding parties, from small barrel rooms to large barns. Venues range from Western theme to elegant, with catering to match. Winery settings provide beautiful backdrops for wedding photographs. The Loma Vista Bed and Breakfast offers a wedding party special for renting multiple rooms. This photograph was taken several years ago at the Cilurzo Winery gazebo, overlooking the pond. Many of the wineries offer meeting rooms and conference rooms to accommodate groups of all sizes.

MARKETING OPPORTUNITIES. Audrey Cilurzo (right) pours a glass for John Hunneman, a well-known columnist for a local newspaper, during an event at the Embassy Suites hotel. To promote business, local winery owners take every opportunity to showcase their products locally and at regional events. These may include local, county, and state fairs and charity events. Often the wineries give away products in hopes they will entice participants to visit their wineries later. Sometimes individual wineries have booths at events like the Balloon and Wine Festivals, and at other times, they join with other wineries to represent the entire Temecula Wine Country. Also, by entering wines in competitions, they are recognized among wine lovers. Hunneman was an enthusiastic participant during the Wine and Cigar Dinners hosted by the Cilurzos and frequently shares news of the Wine Country in his columns. The Temecula Valley Chamber of Commerce awarded the Cilurzos lifetime achievement awards for their contributions to developing the Temecula Wine Country.

RIVERSIDE INTERNATIONAL WINE COMPETITION. The competition had a humble beginning in Temecula Valley when local winery owners and businesspeople met for lunch in 1981. Originally called Farmers Fair Wine Competition, it was run by coordinator Nancy Johnston and Dan Berger, a wine writer for the *San Diego Union* newspaper at the time, who was the head judge. The 250 entries the first year grew to about 2,700 entries today.

SETTING UP FOR JUDGING. Harlan Orrin (left) and other Temecula Valley Wine Society volunteers catalogue each wine and place bottles in the correct class. During the judging, over 70 volunteers pour and serve wine to the judges. The volunteers clear dirty glasses and set up for the next class of wine for judges to taste and evaluate. About 200 wines are entered in each of the smaller Temecula/San Diego competitions.

PREPARING TO POUR. Edna Barnes (left) numbered glasses to correspond with the numbers on bottles, and Sandy Brassard confirmed the numbers matched the bottles. The Riverside International Wine Competition was staffed almost entirely by Temecula Valley Wine Society volunteers. Care is given to check and recheck to make sure the wines judged are labeled and poured correctly. Judges do blind tastings, meaning they know the classification of each wine they taste but do not know which winery made it, in order to give unbiased opinions. After sampling wine, they often spit it into buckets next to the tables and rinse their mouths with water or taste cheese or bread to cleanse their palates. It takes over 100 volunteers to catalogue, store, and deliver over 10,000 bottles of wine for each competition. About 40 judges evaluate the wines.

SERVING WINE TO JUDGE. Harlan Orrin serves judge Mitch Cosentino a tray of wine. Cosentino owns a winery in Northern California. Three volunteers are usually assigned to pour for each of the 12 teams of four judges. Sparkling and white wines are served chilled, and red wine is served at room temperature. Volunteers may take home unused wine from opened bottles, and local nonprofit groups are given unopened bottles to use for fund-raising activities.

JUDGE TASTING WINE. Head judge Dan Berger tastes a glass of red wine. When the wines are received for the competition, they are catalogued and shelved in a cool warehouse to ensure the wines are presented in the most favorable way. Numbers are assigned to each entry by computer and put on the bottles. On the weekend of the competition, wines are packed by class and are taken to the judging site by refrigerated truck.

Four

TODAY'S WINERIES

It took a while to get rolling, but now Temecula wineries are busy seven days a week, and thousands of visitors go in and out of the 30-plus tasting rooms every weekend. The city of Temecula is growing to accommodate all the visitors. Hotels are often near capacity, and two more large hotels are under construction. Destination Temecula, the first touring company to provide Wine Country transportation beginning in 1994, is busier than ever. A handful of bonded wineries make wine but do not have tasting rooms. Wineries range in size from small, family-run operations to a big resort and spa. There are several restaurants and three bed-and-breakfasts in the Wine Country. And if the area in Wine Country is not enough, several tasting rooms are opening in Old Town Temecula.

HART WINERY. The Harts planted their 10 acres in 1974, and by 1980, they made their first wines and opened their winery. This winery has won numerous gold medal and best-of-class awards. They grow Merlot, Fume Blanc, Grenache Rose, Syrah, Sangiovese, Zinfandel, Cabernet Sauvignon, and Cabernet Franc. They produce about 5,000 cases per year. (RFH.)

JOE HART. A third-generation Californian, Joe (right) came to Temecula with his wife, Nancy, and their three sons in the 1970s during the renaissance of the California wine industry. Growing up in a family of teetotalers, he had never tasted wine until he was stationed in the army in southern Germany. Hart now teaches classes and gives lectures about wine and is a sought-after wine judge. The judge on the left is unidentified.

CALLAWAY WINES. Forty years after the opening of the winery, Callaway's legacy for quality continues. In 1976, Queen Elizabeth, not a known drinker, offered a toast at the New York Waldorf-Astoria with a glass of Callaway's 1974 White Riesling. When she finished the glass, she requested another. In 1992, Callaway was an official sponsor of the America's Cup in San Diego. A genius promoter with an innovative approach, Ely Callaway engaged a sales force to put their wines in all the good restaurants in California. Keys to his success were the team of senior vice president John Moramarco and winemaker Dwayne Helmuth. Callaway's affiliation with Allied Domenicq supplied the winery with state-of-the-art equipment and facilities. Present-day gourmet dining is available in the Meritage Restaurant, pairing foods with their fruit-forward wines.

THORNTON WINERY. Nestled in the heart of Temecula Valley Wine Country, this winery, formerly the Culbertson Winery, creates award-winning sparkling and premium varietal wine, including the Méthode Champenoise Champagne and Estate Syrah. The traditional méthode champenoise process is considered best for sparkling wines and champagnes. Utilizing the method with new varieties of grapes produces a classic style wine of the Mediterranean and Rhone regions.

THORNTON FOUNTAIN. Owners John and Sally Thornton offer musical events, including their signature Champagne Jazz Series from April through October, featuring nationally renowned contemporary jazz musicians at the Fountain Terrace. Now celebrating their 20th anniversary, the winery continues to offer premiere food, wine, and musical experiences. Café Champagne is a four-star, award-winning restaurant serving contemporary fusion-style cuisine.

BAILY WINERY. Phil and Carol Baily planted their first vineyard for their family-owned estate winery in 1982. Phil, the winemaker, specializes in Bordeaux varieties of red wines and ages them in oak for 24 to 36 months. He seals his bottles with a synthetic closure called Nomacorc to prevent impurities from corks.

RON ROBERTS AND PHIL BAILY. Former mayor Roberts (left) chats with Baily at Carol's Restaurant at Baily Winery. Carol Baily is executive chef for the restaurant that is open for lunch Wednesdays through Sundays and offers live music on weekends. The Bailys' son Chris serves Temecula wines at his restaurants in Old Town Temecula, Baily's Fine Dining and Front Street Bar and Grill.

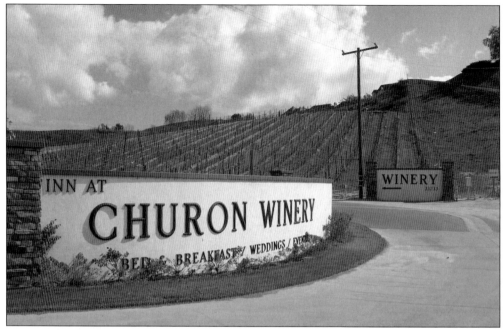

THE CHURON WINERY. The winery produces many varieties of wine but has won more awards for their red wines than their other wines. It is open seven days a week. They offer a five-course wine pairing dinner each Friday and Saturday night. Their 25 bed-and-breakfast rooms have recently been refurbished, and the grounds have recently been relandscaped. (RFH.)

THE INN AT CHURON WINERY. The name Churon was formed from the names of Chuck Johnson and Ron Thomas, who built it. The vineyard was planted in 1998, and the winery was bonded in 2001. The hilltop setting offers wide views for guests at the bed-and-breakfast. The current owners, Ron and Judy Thomas, host weddings in picturesque outdoor venues near a gazebo, small pond and stream, or by one of the two waterfalls. All of the rooms are charmingly furnished with antiques. (MF.)

MIRAMONTE WINERY AND TASTING ROOM. This winery on Rancho California Road was originally founded by Dr. John Piconi. For a short time, Ben Drake's winery and farm management company were there. Since 2001, it has been owned by Cane Vanderhoof and his mother, Sandra Williams, who have created a memorable ambiance in the tasting room. The family-run winery produces 1,000 cases of handcrafted wines annually. (RFH.)

STUART CELLARS VINEYARD AND WINERY. Winemaker Marshall Stuart and his wife, Susan, harvested their first grapes of their 40-acre estate vineyard in 1999. They planted vines in rows running north to south. This French tradition allows even ripening on both sides of the vines and allows the vine to shade the fruit during the heat of the day. They yield about 150 tons of Chardonnay, Merlot, Cabernet Sauvignon, and Cabernet Franc per year and make about 16,000 cases of wine annually. (RFH.)

MOUNT PALOMAR WINES. Mount Palomar Winery is a working wine estate with 40 acres of vineyards. Winemaker Craig Boyd follows the tradition of the winery started by John Poole in 1969. Joe Cherpin, their first winemaker, came from an early Southern California winemaking family and introduced the port and the popular Solera Cream Sherry to the winery. Etienne Cowper was the second winemaker. Until recently, the winery was managed by John's son Peter.

MOUNT PALOMAR WINERY. When John Poole established the winery estate, he created a place where people could immerse themselves in the world of fine wine in a pleasant and relaxed atmosphere. Their wines have been named "Best Wine of the Southern California Region" by the California State Fair five times. They have also been recognized for sustainable environmental practices in viticulture. The winery offers live music and Mediterranean barbecues during weekends.

ALEX'S RED BARN WINERY. Alex and Lise Yakut open their tasting room on Calle Contento to customers on Saturdays and Sundays. They concentrate on making premium wines that include Old Vine Sauvignon Blanc, Old Vine Cabernet Sauvignon, Old Vine Johannesburg Riesling, Solera-style sherry, Viognier, and Syrah. They have won many gold and silver awards at international wine competitions. Their signature wine is Alex's Solera, a cream sherry.

ALEX'S RED BARN TASTING ROOM. The Yakuts manage their 25-acre family estate vineyard with organic pest control measures and have a unique automatic sensor that analyzes soil moisture every five minutes. Alex, a retired aerospace engineer, planted their first vineyard in DeLuz in 1984. He was secretary for the Temecula Growers Association and wrote "The Vine," the association newsletter. He helped integrate the growers and wineries into the Temecula Winegrowers Association.

Falkner Winery. Their first vineyards were planted in 1975. They offer red, white, and rose wines to buy by the case or bottle to enjoy in their picnic area or at home. Steve Hadaka, their winemaker, has made wine for Piconi, Maurice Car'rie, and Temecula Crest in the past. This is a popular wedding venue.

Loretta and Ray Falkner. Elegant dining is available at Pinnacle Restaurant, which opened in 2006 and was named Best Restaurant 2008 by the *Inland Empire Magazine*. A more intimate dining experience is available in the Wine Cave, the barrel room. Other events include monthly wine appreciation classes and wine dinners. The Falkner Winery was previously known as Britton Cellars, Clos du Muriel, and Temecula Crest Wineries.

early spring '91 ... VIEWED from the South

LUMINIERE WINERY. In 1987, Dr. Ezra and Martha Kleiner bought the Barlin family vineyard that was planted with Sauvignon Blanc grapes in 1980. Dr. Kleiner, a Los Angeles pathologist, named the property Martha's Vineyard on Calle Contento. After studying viticulture at UC Davis, he and his wife and children worked in the vineyard, pruning, wrapping, tying, and suckering the vines. For the last five years, their son Andrew has managed the vineyard and started making wine.

BELLA VISTA WINERY. When Imre and Gizella Cziraki bought the Cilurzo Winery in 2004, it was a continuation of a long interest Imre had in wine making. Born in Hungary, Imre began making wine at age seven with his grandfather. The Czirakis produce white and red wines and champagne, specializing in Viognier, Cabernet Sauvignon, and Cabernet Franc. All their farming is organic. (RFH.)

LONGSHADOW RANCH, VINEYARD, AND WINERY. This winery carries out an old-time Western theme in all it does, including the names of its wines, for example, Reata Red, Ponderosa Port, White Feather Chardonnay, and Outlaw Red. Their chocolate port is noteworthy. They have a comfortable picnic area and a tasting room on Calle Contento. Just recently, they opened a tasting room in Old Town Temecula, where they also offer live music. (RFH.)

CARRIAGE RIDE. The Belgian draft horses that pull carriages through the vineyards also work in the vineyards. It is described by visitors as eclectic, rustic, and off the beaten track, and most agree it has country charm. Horseback riding and bonfires are available in this child-friendly atmosphere. This also makes a romantic venue for weddings. Their 26 acres of vineyards, some planted in 1999, produce about 15,000 cases of wine annually.

BRIAR ROSE WINERY. The vineyard was planted in 1995, the winery was bonded in 2002, and it was opened to the public in 2007. This is the first reservation-only boutique winery and tasting room in Temecula, where wine tasting takes place in a fairy tale setting amid beautifully landscaped grounds. A contractor named Beldon Fields designed the cottage in the 1970s to resemble Snow White's cottage in Disneyland.

LES AND DORIAN LINKOGLE AT BRIAR ROSE. The Linkogles invite the public to "taste the enchantment" in their Olde World Tasting Room. Briar Rose Winery is known for its world-class Cabernet Sauvignon, Estate Zinfandel, Petit Verdot, and Aleatico Port. On Sunday afternoons, they have wine education by their staff sommelier. Their wines have been served in the White House and in the Playboy Mansion.

MAURICE CAR'RIE WINERY. The winery, founded by Maurice and Budd Von Roekel in 1986, is now owned by Buddy and Cheri Linn. With winemaker Gus Vizgirda, they handcraft 14 varietals that have received hundreds of awards and accolades. They have pleasant picnic grounds and sell food, including their famous baked Brie and sourdough bread. (RFH.)

VICTORIAN FARMHOUSE. The signature architecture of this winery is the Victorian farmhouse that gives a homey feel to the grounds. They offer multiple venues for private dining, banquets, and conferences, including the 100-year-old barn. Each weekend, crafters set up booths to sell wares that include jewelry, purses, and other handmade items.

LA CEREZA VINEYARD AND WINERY. Winemaker Gus Vizgirda produces premium boutique wines in small quantities that have won awards, including the Best Viognier in the State of California and the Best Red Grenache in Temecula Valley. They also make Girlfriends, the first wine produced in Southern California to appeal to female palates. They are also known for their raspberry champagne. Their hand-numbered labels are works of art and feature stories on the back label. (RFH.)

SPECIALTY WINES. Buddy and Cheri Linn, the current owners, have transformed the former Von Roekel Winery to reflect a Spanish, Mediterranean look. La Cereza is Spanish for "cherry." They present La Cereza and Von Roekel wines in a tasting room decorated with changing exhibits of art. The unique Hemingways Wine and Cigar Bar is open on weekends as weather permits.

SOUTH COAST WINERY, RESORT, AND SPA. Jim Carter, transplanted from a cold Ohio, now immerses himself in Southern California sunshine and verdant vineyards daily. The 1990s movie *A Walk in the Clouds* inspired him to follow his dream to develop a winery and to share the serenity of the setting with strangers. This is a beautiful wedding venue.

BEST WINERY IN CALIFORNIA, 2008. The South Coast Winery Resort won this prestigious Golden Bear Award for its luxurious resort and fine service. Freestanding deluxe villas are up to 1,100 square feet in size and have fireplaces, spa tubs, and private terraces. The resort is set up to give guests a total Wine Country experience.

VINEYARD ROSE RESTAURANT. The resort offers a wide variety of dishes for breakfast, lunch, and dinner, expertly prepared by a chef. There are also ample meeting rooms with catering available for groups of any size. South Coast wines are served in the restaurant and at a tasting bar. These may include Sweet Maggie and Black Jack Port, made by winemaker Jon McPherson.

JIM CARTER AND HIS GRAPES. Couples or individuals wanting to pamper themselves during a weekend getaway can get massages at the Grape Seed Spa. Vine-based treatments are offered for skin care and relaxation. A state-of-the-art fitness center and a full-service beauty salon are also available.

LOMA VISTA BED AND BREAKFAST. *Los Angeles Times* food editor Elmer Dills helped put Temecula on the map when he discovered the bed-and-breakfast in the late 1980s, shortly after it was built by Dick and Betty Ryan. The inn offers 10 guest rooms, a 10-person outdoor Jacuzzi tub, free limousine service, and full gourmet breakfasts. Patios give beautiful views of the valley. (PG, VN.)

KARL AND CONNIE SWEIGART. The Sweigarts, who bought Loma Vista in 2006, entertain guests from all over the world. Surprisingly most visitors come from a 100-mile radius of Temecula to enjoy a weekend getaway in the Wine Country. Their rooms are each decorated differently and bear the names of popular wines. The Sweigarts offer a weekend wedding package that includes a private honeymoon suite. (PG, VN.)

PONTE WINERY. Brothers Roberto and Claudio Ponte, Temecula grape growers since 1984, built the Ponte Family Estate Winery in the heart of the Wine Country, amid 350 acres of the former Brookside vineyards. Most of the 30-year-old vines on the property produce Cabernet, Merlot, and Chardonnay. They also grow Zinfandel, Sangiovese, and Muscat. Winemaker Robert Cartwright directs production of 15,000 cases of wine annually.

THE SMOKEHOUSE RESTAURANT. Guests enjoy lunch at the all-outdoor dining patio, feasting on superb Wine Country cuisine made with local, fresh ingredients designed to enhance Ponte Family Estate wines. The winery also offers catering, a tasting room, a vineyard pavilion and banquet facility, and wedding gardens. A mission-style building serves as a cellar and barrel room.

WIENS FAMILY CELLARS. The Wiens produce a broad range of gold medal–winning wines from their estate-farmed varietals and are known for their "Big Reds" and sparkling Amour De L'Orange. Their mission is to produce the highest quality wine and to provide it at a reasonable price. Each October, they offer a Wienfest event with their wines, craft beers, German food and music, and a grape stomp.

WIENS FAMILY. The Wiens are, from left to right, Jeff, Dave, Mary, Doug, and George. Doug Wiens, winemaker and viticulturist, says the family enjoys spending time together and making wine is a family thing, often involving the extended family of up to 46 people. (JH.)

PALUMBO FAMILY VINEYARD. Dormant vines give a clear view to the snowy mountains beyond Palumbo Family Vineyards and Winery. The Palumbos grow Cabernet, Sauvignon, Cabernet Franc, Merlot, and Sangiovese varietals on the 13-acre property planted in 1991 and 1999. They specialize in small-lot, handcrafted wines from the varieties grown. The family-run winery produces 2,500 cases of artisan wines per year. This winery, bonded in 2002, is known for their full-bodied reds.

DURING THE CRUSH, 2004. Nick and Cindy Palumbo smile over their good harvest as they rake grapes into the crusher. Their children Reed, Ryan, Sophia, and Dominick help them with work in the vineyard. Focusing on wines, they offer few events, which include private wine dinners for 8 to 16 people. They offer a popular Meritage called Tre Fratelli and a 2005 Shiraz/Cabernet Sauvignon.

WILSON CREEK WINERY. The Temecula Valley Chamber of Commerce named the Wilson Creek Winery the Golden Business of the Year in 2007 in recognition of the many charity events they host for the community. The winery holds fund-raisers for many organizations each year, including ones to help children with autism and juvenile diabetes. (RFH.)

WILSON CREEK TASTING ROOM. The Wilsons' most popular product is their Almond Champagne. Etienne Cowper, their winemaker, also makes Chocolate Port, Anglica Cream Sherry, and other wines. The winery offers venues for conferences and weddings. The open-air Creekside Grill serves from 11:00 a.m. to 5:00 p.m. every day. (RFH.)

LEGACY. This label honors Gerry and Rosie Wilson, who founded the family business. It states, "Rosie and Gerry Wilson have a dynamic impact on numerous people and are leaving a profound impact on their family and many others that will last from generation to generation. They have imprinted on many hearts, immediate family and extended family alike, a legacy of grace, compassion, faith, humor, dependability, character and love." (RFH.)

GRAND OPENING. From left to right, the following Wilsons (in light-colored clothing) pose with two unidentified representatives of the Temecula Chamber of Commerce: Craig, Rosie, Libby, Gerry, Jenifer, Mick, and Bill. The entire family works at the winery in one capacity or another. This was taken during their grand opening in October 2000.

THE CASTLE BED AND BREAKFAST.
Visitors to Wine Country may want
to try the Castle Bed and Breakfast
for a good "knight's sleep." This inn
is designed as an escape from the
everyday world. Inside it is decorated
in a romantically European decor,
offering four distinctly different Old
World, country-style designs. (MF.)

LOUIS AND SHERRY DiBERNARDO. The
DiBernardos, owners and proprietors of
the Castle Bed and Breakfast, welcome
guests to relax and converse in the
Great Room in the evening over a glass
of wine, port, or sherry. The rooms
are decorated in Venetian, Medieval,
French Country, and English Tudor
styles. The inn is also available for
weddings, private parties, and concerts.

DOFFO WINERY. Marcelo Doffo owns this vineyard that was planted in 1999 and winery that was bonded in 2004. He attributes his healthy vine growth to the infusion of love and classical music they are given. Doffo produces about 950 cases of handcrafted wines annually. He specializes in red wine, and his Private Reserve Cabernet Sauvignon is one of his premium wines.

HYATT SCHOOL. The historical one-room school is a cornerstone to the Doffo Winery property. It served as a school and community meeting place in the late 1800s and early 1900s before being moved to its present location, where it is not currently used. Doffo also has a vintage motorcycle collection available for viewing.

FOOTE PRINT WINERY. This small winery on the east side of the Temecula Wine Country produces simple, no-frills red wines from the vineyard planted in 2001. They were bonded in 2005 and produce about 800 cases per year. Their estate grapes are certified organic. Their tasting room and gift store are open Friday through Sunday and by appointment. (RFH.)

IN THE FOOTE PRINT VINEYARD. Deane and Christine Foote own and operate this vineyard, organic farm, and small winery. Deane is the winemaker. Their Foote Path Farms grow a variety of fruits that are available year-round. Their wine club is called Club Foote.

FILSINGER VINEYARDS AND WINERY. William and Katharine Filsinger purchased 35 acres of vineyard property in 1978 that had been planted with Zinfandel and Sauvignon Blanc grapes in 1972, and they opened a winery in 1980. William left his medical practice in Orange County to devote his time to wine making and became successful at it. He planted the first Gewürztraminer grapes in Southern California, and his wine from these grapes is his most popular. (RFH.)

THE FILSINGERS. William's parents immigrated to Ohio from Mainz, Germany, after World War I. His grandparents owned and operated a winery in Germany that was later confiscated by the Nazis. The Filsingers produce about 3,000 cases of red, white, rose, and sparkling wine per year. Their tasting room is open Friday through Sunday, and they have a room with a kitchen available to rent for events. (RFH.)

OAK MOUNTAIN WINES. Picturesque hillside vineyards were planted in 2000 and 2005 with classic Bordeaux varieties of Cabernet Franc, Merlot, Petite Verdot, Malbec, and Cabernet Sauvignon. They have also slipped in some unique varietals such as Counoise and Pinotage. The winery was licensed in 2006 and is the only Temecula Valley winery that houses two labels under one roof. Their other label is Temecula Hills Winery.

VALERIE AND STEPHEN ANDREWS. Oak Mountain Winery, originally named Windy Ridge Cellars, is located off a dirt road at an elevation of 2,900 feet overlooking Diamond Valley Lake and with views of Oak Mountain. They grow Rhone-style varietals. Their flagship wine is their Tempranillo, and one of the most popular is their Cabernet Sauvignon. Stephen is the winemaker, and Valerie oversees all other operations.

TEMECULA HILLS. Stephen Andrews also makes Temecula Hills wines, which can be tasted in the Oak Mountain Winery tasting rooms in Wine Country and in Old Town Country. Ed's Red has a sweet cherry aroma and flavors of pepper, spice, black cherry, and roasted nut. Stephen and Valerie suggest it as an accompaniment to beef or lamb dishes or to chocolate desserts.

TEMECULA HILLS TEMPRANILLO HARVEST. The tempranillo grape, the most pedigreed red grape of Spain, is especially associated with the historic Rioja region. It is a dark, lush fruit that ages well to an intensely ripe fruit flavor. It pairs well with paella, other rice or grain dishes, or lamb or other fragrant meats.

MASIA DE YABAR. Wilmer and Silvia Yabar's Mediterranean-style winery on Camino Arroyo Seco, off De Portola Road, brings a Spanish ambiance to Temecula. The name of the winery means "the manor house," comes from the era of feudal lords, and is indicative of a strongly constructed shelter where everyone is welcome to enjoy "the good life." The Spanish wines produced from the vineyard planted in July 2007 include Tempranillo Grenache and Monastrele Ralbec. The winery was bonded in September 2007 and is open every day from 11:00 a.m. to 5:00 p.m. Wilmer, originally from Peru, brings to the Temecula Valley his exclusive experience in the wine fields of Argentina. Their wines are dry and full-bodied, with notes of black currant, plum, and soft tannins. The winery building is available for special events. (RFH.)

COUGAR VINEYARD AND WINERY. This winery, bonded in 2004, specializes in Italian varietals. Owners and winemakers Rick and Jennifer Buffington named the winery for Cougar Mountain in Bellevue, Washington, where they lived previously. They produce about 3,000 cases per year. The Buffingtons invite wine lovers to come visit, meet their dogs, and enjoy their serene setting surrounded by olive trees and roses with stunning views of the vineyards. (RFH.)

FRANGIPANI ESTATE VINEYARDS AND WINERY. Don and JoAnn Frangipani own the Spanish villa–style estate winery on DePortola Road. They offer a rural setting among olive trees for romantic weddings, small equestrian events, and country barbecues. They are known for their red wines. They produce about 4,000 cases of Voignier, Sauvignon Blanc, and Grenache Rose each year. (RFH.)

LEONNESE CELLARS. The name of the winery means "Village of Dreams," and owners Gary and Lana Winder and Mike and Lisa Rennie hope everyone who visits will be carried into a dream world with moments enjoyed there with family and friends. They offer lawn and terrace areas that seat up to 300 people for weddings and other ceremonies. The vineyard was planted in 1999, and the winery was bonded in 2003.

VINEYARD VIEW FROM LEONNESE PATIO. This setting offers wide views of Palomar Mountain and 70 acres of estate vineyards and horse properties, an inviting place for patio gatherings. Leonnese offers Winemaker Dinners, grape stomping, and barrel tasting. They specialize in Rhone varieties and blends. Their red wines have been awarded numerous Double Gold Medal and 90 Point ratings in major wine review publications. The Rennies plan a new tasting room in Old Town Temecula.

Keyways Vineyard and Winery. Formerly owned by Carl Keys, the original vineyard was planted with Zinfandel and Grenache as an experimental vineyard. The winery was bonded in 1990. In 2006, current owner Terri Lee Delhamer replanted and expanded the vineyards, adding Tempranillo, Viognier, and Roussanne. From estate wines, they make a white Rhone blend and are known for their Tempranillo, Zinfandel, and Krystal Ice Wine.

Terri Lee Pedley Delhamer and Award-Winning Wines. Keyways is the only female-owned and -managed winery in Temecula Valley. Delhamer has developed a warm and charming tasting room serviced by a friendly and knowledgeable staff. She offers unique events, including the TGIF at Keyways Piano Bar and Acoustical Guitar Sangria Sundays. During her annual Temeculights Holiday Lighting Festival–Wine Country Cowboy Christmas, guests are treated to horse-drawn wagon rides through the vineyards.

CURRY FAMILY. Charlie and Michele Curry run a small, family-owned boutique winery, where they make handcrafted wine from their vineyards. They credit their success to their vigilant quality control from bud through bottling. This is a bonded winery that does not have a tasting room, but their wines can be purchased online.

CURRY VINEYARDS. The Currys practice organic methods of pest control with composting and fertilizer. This photograph shows Charlie spraying phylox sulfur, an organic compound, to control powdery mildew. They produce Petite Sirah and Cabernet Sauvignon. They planted in 2000 and were bonded in 2005.

ROBERT RENZONI VINEYARDS. The Renzoni family started making wine in Italy in 1886. Robert and his parents moved to Temecula in 2004. They purchased the vineyard property on DePortola Road and added more vines in 2006. The tasting room is at one end of their wine-making facility and another is planned for the property.

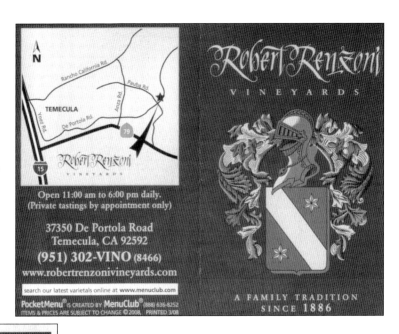

Boorman Vineyards & Estate Winery
21630 Avenida De Arboles
Murrieta, Ca. 92562   951-600-9333

So. Cal's Premium Red Wine Producer

BOORMAN VINEYARDS ESTATE WINERY. This private estate winery owned by Todd and Rosie Boorman since 1986 is located on Avenida del Arboles in Murrieta on the Santa Rosa Plateau. Their original vineyard was planted in 1978. They were bonded in 2002 and produce about 1,000 cases per years, specializing in red Bordeaux varietals, including a blended wine they call Metaphor. They are open for tastings and tours for special events and by appointment.

TESORO WINERY. This tasting room with a Tuscan ambience at the corner of Old Town Front Street and Sixth Street in Old Town Temecula is open after the Wine Country tasting rooms close. They are open until 7:00 p.m. Sundays through Thursdays and until 9:00 p.m. on Fridays and Saturdays. Every Saturday evening, they offer a celebration of good wine and live music during their Sabato Sera Musica. Etienne Cowper is their winemaker. (RFH.)

VILLA DI CALABRO. This house on Main Street in Old Town will soon offer wine tasting rooms for Villa di Calabro and Temecula Hills Wineries and an olive oil tasting room for Calabro olive products. Villa di Calabro is owned by Mike Calabro and Mindy Cooke. Both Mike and Mindy are longtime members of the Temecula Valley Wine Society. (RFH.)

TEMECULA HOUSE OF WINE. Temecula House of Wine is located in the Palomar Inn in Old Town Temecula, and owner Carlos Palma loves wine and Old Town Temecula. In December 2004, it occurred to him that he could combine his two passions by selling wine in his Palomar Inn hotel in Old Town, where patrons can purchase many of Temecula's award-winning wines. The inn, a historical landmark, has been in the Majeski/Palma family for over 60 years. (RFH.)

LONGSHADOW TASTING ROOM. Longshadow has opened a tasting room in Old Town Temecula to reach people who are not going into the Wine Country. Old Town is redefined with two trendy restaurants and a live theater. The hundreds of visitors who come to Old Town can enjoy a taste of the Wine Country. (RFH.)

Monument in Wine Country. This monument on Rancho California Road welcomes visitors to the Wine Country. Bonded wineries that do not have tasting rooms include Atwood, Chapin, Cowper, Rey Sol, Gershon Bachus, Las Piedras, Monte de Oro, Olive View, Santa Maria, SC Cellars, Villa Vesia, Peltzer, and Hawk Watch. Retail outlets that carry local wines include Barons, Temecula Valley Wine Company, BevMo, Stellar Cellar, and CVS. (RFH.)

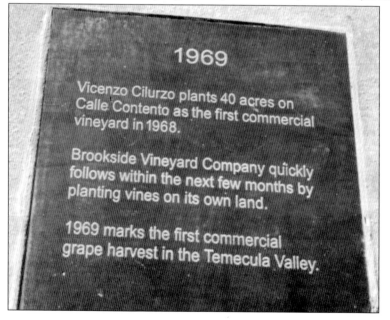

1969

Vicenzo Cilurzo plants 40 acres on Calle Contento as the first commercial vineyard in 1968.

Brookside Vineyard Company quickly follows within the next few months by planting vines on its own land.

1969 marks the first commercial grape harvest in the Temecula Valley.

Library Timeline. The planting of the Cilurzo Vineyard in 1969 is noted on the historic timeline at the Temecula Public Library as an event that changed the course of Temecula history. It almost did not happen, and the vineyard almost did not make it through the first growing season. It did succeed, and now thousands of people visit Temecula and the wines are enjoyed all over the world.

THE CILURZO FAMILY, 1982. From left to right, Chenin, Audrey, Vincenzo, and Vinnie pose in the barrel room. Chenin and Vinnie grew up helping their parents in the vineyard and winery. Little did they realize they would become a part of wine history. The village of Temecula became a city in 1989, and it has become a tourist destination. There are 30-plus wineries in the valley. New vineyards are being planted, more wineries and restaurants are planned, and new hotels are under construction. Vincenzo retired from television lighting. In 2004 he and Audrey sold their winery and live locally. Both are still active in the Temecula Wine Society and wine competitions. Chenin and her husband, Sean Carlton, have a winery in Oregon (www.basketcasewine.com). Vinnie and his wife, Natalie, have a production brewery and brewpub in Santa Rosa, California (www.russianriverbrewing.com). In 1968, when Vincenzo and Audrey planted Temecula's first vineyard, they had the vision to see that Temecula would become an important wine region.

ACROSS AMERICA, PEOPLE ARE DISCOVERING SOMETHING WONDERFUL. *THEIR HERITAGE.*

Arcadia Publishing is the leading local history publisher in the United States. With more than 5,000 titles in print and hundreds of new titles released every year, Arcadia has extensive specialized experience chronicling the history of communities and celebrating America's hidden stories, bringing to life the people, places, and events from the past. To discover the history of other communities across the nation, please visit:

www.arcadiapublishing.com

Customized search tools allow you to find regional history books about the town where you grew up, the cities where your friends and family live, the town where your parents met, or even that retirement spot you've been dreaming about.